MW00975413

COACH

COACH

A Treasury of Inspiration and Laughter

Jess Brallier

Sally Chabert

CB

CONTEMPORARY BOOKS

Library of Congress Cataloging-in-Publication Data

Brallier, Jess M.
    Coach : a treasury of inspiration and laughter / Jess Brallier and
Sally Chabert.
        p.   cm.
    ISBN 0-8092-2589-1
    1. Coaching (Athletics)—Quotations, maxims, etc.   2. Coaches
(Athletics) Quotations.   3. Sports Quotations, maxims, etc.
I. Chabert, Sally.   II. Title.
PN6084.C54B73   2000
796'.07'7—dc21   99-23271
                                                                  CIP

Interior design by Nick Panos
Interior illustrations by Dan Krovatin

Published by Contemporary Books
A division of NTC/Contemporary Publishing Group, Inc.
4255 West Touhy Avenue, Lincolnwood (Chicago), Illinois 60712-1975 U.S.A.
Copyright © 2000 by Jess Brallier and Sally Chabert
Printed in the United States of America
International Standard Book Number: 0-8092-2589-1

00 01 02 03 04 LB 19 18 17 16 15 14 13 12 11 10 9 8 7 6 5 4 3 2 1

To Leigh and Doug,
Stoecker and Sector

Believe nothing, no matter where you read it, or who said it—even if I have said it—unless it agrees with your own reason and your own common sense.

The Buddha

Foreword

Coaches, trust me when I tell you that this is one very unique book.

That's because, of the millions of books that have been published over the centuries, this is certainly the only one in which you'll find a quote from Paul "Bear" Bryant, the legendary Alabama football coach, immediately following a quote from Henry David Thoreau, the great American essayist, poet, and philosopher. In my mind, any one book that can combine the thoughts of those two great gentlemen—and do it on the same page—is right on the money.

I found myself pouring through page after page of this extraordinary work. As a coach, I'm always looking for just the right quote, just the right observation, just the right statement to make to my teams as they're preparing to go out and give 100 percent on game day. And in *Coach*, I have finally found the perfect source.

Jess Brallier and Sally Chabert have done a magnificent job of compiling these compelling quotes and observations from all over. You'll find yourself, as I have, referring to the pages again and again. This is one of those books that you'll want to keep close by on your bookshelf, because for a coach, it's an instant reference source of just what to say and how to say it. Even better, the quotes are downright entertaining.

So, Coach, the next time you want to inspire and motivate your players and you don't know where to start, reach for this book first. You may not coach like a Vince Lombardi or a Phil Jackson, but at least you'll sound like one.

RICK WOLFF

Wolff is a nationally recognized expert in the field of sports psychology. His written work is often seen in *Sports Illustrated* and in *Sports Illustrated for Kids*, and he's the host of "The Sports Edge," a weekly sports parenting program on WFAN radio in New York City. His latest book is *Coaching Kids for Dummies* (IDG Books).

A Note to the Reader

We congratulate you, the coach.

On almost any day of the year, as we drive or walk about the neighborhood, we see you. We watch you struggle with heavy equipment bags, work the phones, and line the playing fields. We see you encourage, cheer, discipline, and laugh. We see you over at the hockey rink at 5 A.M., at the town's lighted basketball courts at 10 P.M., and in between, at the Little League, soccer, and Pop Warner fields.

You are one of more than two million volunteers who annually coach more than 20 million boys and girls. We know you well. Although we've been the coach, we've more often been the appreciative parents of one of your charges.

We think you deserve your own book.

Coach is to be *enjoyed*, either leafed through or read from beginning to end; at one or one hundred sittings; alone or among friends; at courtside or poolside; with or without whistle.

The book is loosely structured around the three themes common to all your coaching seasons: Preparation, Competition, and After the Game.

This collection is more for volunteer coaches—moms and dads and neighbors—than it is for the professional coach. You are more likely to be part father, part grocer, and part Little League coach, than Phil Jackson or Bill Parcells.

Because coaching and sports is really about all of life, we've drawn upon many lives, from Erma Bombeck, Anne Frank, Mel Brooks, and the Duke of Wellington to Vince Lombardi, Lou Holtz, Mary Lou Retton, and Casey Stengel. This variety also provides for the proven joy of juxtaposition—an Oscar Wilde quote immediately followed by a Mike Ditka quote, Thomas Jefferson paired with Lou Brock, and William Shakespeare next to Joe Namath.

The quotes here are as universal as possible, in every way possible; not limited to baseball, not limited to the male coach. In compiling this collection, we drew not only upon a library of sports and inspirational resources but also upon the unexpected, such as a movie (*Air Bud*), television (*Alf*), historical and world figures (Abraham

Lincoln and Winston Churchill), and literature (James Baldwin and Anne Morrow Lindbergh).

This is not a reference book with entries like "defense," "quitters," "injuries," or "halftime." Because the real value of this collection is in the words—and not the profession of whoever first took credit for saying the words—a quotation's source is identified only by name. However, should you be curious, an index of sources with attributes is provided.

In *Coach*, we hope you find the inspiration and laughter to endure, reflect, and renew. You certainly deserve it.

COACH

Preparation

Failure to prepare is preparing to fail.

John Wooden

If people knew how hard I have had to work to gain my mastery, it wouldn't seem so wonderful.

Michelangelo

The Battle of Waterloo was won on the playing fields of Eton.

Duke of Wellington

Everything comes to him who hustles while he waits.

Thomas A. Edison

Do something every day that you don't want to do;
this is the golden rule for acquiring the habit of doing
your duty without pain.

Mark Twain

I have seen hard work beat good luck seven days a
week.

Maurice "Mo" Vaughn

A great part of courage is the courage of having done
the thing before.

Ralph Waldo Emerson

You play the way you practice.

Glenn Scobey "Pop" Warner

You may be disappointed if you fail, but you are doomed if you don't try.

Beverly Sills

Winning can be defined as the science of being totally prepared.

George Allen

All things at first appear difficult.

Chinese proverb

Champions aren't made in gyms. Champions are made from something they have deep inside them—a desire, a dream, a vision. They have to have last-minute stamina, they have to be a little faster, they have to have the skill and the will. But the will must be stronger than the skill.

Muhammad Ali

COACHING... WHY?

A teacher affects eternity; he can never tell where his influence stops.

Henry Adams

I always turn to the sports page first. The sports page records people's accomplishments; the front page has nothing but man's failures.

Earl Warren

There are only two lasting bequests we can hope to give our children. One of these is roots, the other, wings.

Hodding Carter

Games lubricate the body and the mind.

Benjamin Franklin

I want to forget the instructional tapes and the clinics
and the winter talk about summer tournaments . . . but
feel, instead, the delight when you put all your
strength and happiness in being young and strong into
a swing, and the ball rises above the grass where it can
skid past the trees and disappear into the bushes.

Mel Allen

Sports do not build character. They reveal it.

Heywood Hale Broun

To give without any reward, or any notice, has a
special quality of its own.

Anne Morrow Lindbergh

Strive for excellence, not perfection.

H. Jackson Brown Jr.

No pain, no balm; no thorns, no throne; no gall, no glory; no cross, no crown.

William Penn

The key is not the "will to win" . . . everybody has that. It is the will to prepare to win that is important.

Bobby Knight

Do what you can, with what you have, where you are.

Theodore Roosevelt

Sometimes it is more important to discover what one cannot do, than what one can do.

Lin Yü-t'ang

Preparation prevents piss-poor performance.

Nolan Richardson

Effort measures success better than outcome.

Anonymous

You've got to be in position for luck to happen. Luck doesn't go around looking for a stumblebum.

Darrell Royal

An ounce of application is worth a ton of abstraction.

Booker T. Washington

The biggest dog has been a pup.

Joaquin Miller

It is never too late to be what you might have been.

George Eliot

I was the school's worst athlete. I could not catch or throw. I could barely run. I struck out seven straight times when I played baseball. From sports I learned that I was never going to be wonderful. I learned to be satisfied with small matters, getting, for example, into a football game for three plays. Sports taught me that my days were going to be ordinary, and instead of dreaming about the extraordinary and faraway, I learned to appreciate, and love, the familial and the neighborly.

Sam Pickering

The quality of a person's life is in direct proportion to their commitment to excellence, regardless of their chosen field of endeavor.

Vince Lombardi

Failure is the path of least persistence.

Michael Larsen

The problem with many athletes is they take themselves seriously and their sport lightly.

Mike Newlin

Confidence is the result of hours and days and weeks and years of constant work and dedication.

Roger Staubach

Forget goals. Value the process.

Jim Bouton

When people keep telling you that you can't do a thing, you kind of like to try it.

Margaret Chase Smith

No coach ever won a game by what he knows; it's what his players have learned.

Paul "Bear" Bryant

KIDS

Children have more need of models than of critics.

Joseph Joubert

People who get nostalgic about childhood were obviously never children.

Bill Watterson

Children today are tyrants. They contradict their parents, gobble their food, and tyrannize their teachers.

Socrates

Till I was thirteen, I thought my name was "Shut Up."

Joe Namath

The secret of dealing successfully with a child is not to be its parent.

Mel Lazarus

I've seen kids ride bicycles, run, play ball, set up a camp, swing, fight a war, swim, and race for eight hours . . . yet have to be driven to the garbage can.

Erma Bombeck

Don't follow trends, start trends.

Frank Capra

Sweat plus sacrifice equals success.

Charles Finley

If a man is called to be a streetsweeper, he should sweep streets even as Michelangelo painted, or Beethoven composed music, or Shakespeare wrote poetry. He should sweep streets so well that all the hosts of heaven and earth will pause to say, here lived a great streetsweeper who did his job well.

Martin Luther King Jr.

Genius: It's 1 percent inspiration and 99 percent perspiration. No one has ever drowned in sweat.

Lou Holtz

You should be able to do your entire routine sound asleep in your pajamas without one mistake.

Mary Lou Retton

It's a good idea to obey all the rules when you're young just so you'll have the strength to break them when you're old.

Mark Twain

Build your team a feeling of oneness, of dependence on one another, and of strength to be derived by unity.

Vince Lombardi

There are two kinds of worries—those you can do something about and those you can't. Don't spend any time on the latter.

Duke Ellington

Don't fight the problem, decide it.

George C. Marshall

The graveyards are full of indispensable men.

Charles de Gaulle

A spoonful of honey will catch more flies than a gallon of vinegar.

Benjamin Franklin

When angry, count ten before you speak; if very angry, one hundred.

Thomas Jefferson

If you step on people in this life, you're going to come back as a cockroach.

Willie Davis

Always be a little kinder than necessary.

James M. Barrie

Climb high
Climb far
Your goal the sky
Your aim the star

Anonymous

I learned that a great leader is a man who has the
ability to get other people to do what they don't want
to do and like it.

Harry S. Truman

I'm not interested in what these kids *can't* do, I'm
interested in what they *can* do.

Bill Hankins

MORE OF KIDS

Explain the concept of death very carefully to a child.
This will make threatening him with it much more
effective.

P. J. O'Rourke

The ultimate cool is not being concerned, it's not
worrying about whether you are cool or not.

Bruce Willis

When you are eight years old, nothing is any of your business.

Lenny Bruce

The best way to give advice to your children is to find out what they want and then advise them to do it.

Harry S. Truman

Children have never been very good at listening to their elders, but they have never failed to imitate them.

James Baldwin

The difficult we do immediately. The impossible takes a little longer.

Slogan of the U.S. Army Service Forces

The key to developing people is to catch them doing something right.

Ken Blanchard and Spencer Johnson

Vested authority. If you can't win the approval of your players, you lose your job. I think the less you control them, the more innovative they can be.

Phil Jackson

Am I not destroying my enemies when I make friends of them?

Abraham Lincoln

Discipline is the soul of an army. It makes small numbers formidable, procures success to the weak and esteem to all.

George Washington

I never thought about being a writer as I grew up; a writer wasn't something to be. An outfielder was something to be. Most of what I know about style I learned from Roberto Clemente.

John Sayles

It is better to wear out than to rust out.

Richard Cumberland

The only way to avoid being miserable is not to have enough leisure to wonder whether you are happy or not.

George Bernard Shaw

THE COACH'S CORNER

Make a kid feel stupid and he'll act stupider.

John Holt

In certain trying circumstances, urgent circumstances, desperate circumstances, profanity furnishes a relief denied even to prayer.

Mark Twain

Don't park in the spaces marked "Reserved for Umpires."

John McSherry

Like my old skleenball coach used to say, find out what you don't do well, then don't do it.

Alf

When the child is twelve, your wife buys her a splendidly silly article of clothing called a training bra. To train *what*? I never had a training *jock*.

Bill Cosby

The secret of managing is to keep the guys who hate you away from the guys who are undecided.

Casey Stengel

The buck stops here.

Harry S. Truman

If you want a place in the sun, you have to expect a few blisters.

Loretta Young

Life is like a sewer—you get out of it what you put into it.

Tom Lehrer

The price of greatness is responsibility.

Winston Churchill

I think there is only one quality worse than hardness of heart, and that is softness of head.

Theodore Roosevelt

Don't let the same dog bite you twice.

Chuck Berry

Keep winning and losing in perspective.
Lead by example.
Go for respect over popularity.
Value character as well as ability.
Work hard but enjoy what you do.

Don Shula

Don't compromise yourself. You are all you've got.

Janis Joplin

A man who has no imagination has no wings.

Muhammad Ali

He who walks in another's tracks leaves no footprints.

Helen Ottway

Nothing great was ever achieved without enthusiasm.

Ralph Waldo Emerson

The difference between a successful person and others is not a lack of strength, not a lack of knowledge, but rather a lack of will.

Vince Lombardi

People always worry about the grass being greener on the other side of the fence. But you should be watering the grass on your side of the fence.

Emmitt Smith

Our life is frittered away by detail . . . simplify, simplify.

Henry David Thoreau

When we have a good team at Alabama, I know it's because we have boys who come from good mamas and papas.

Paul "Bear" Bryant

Better three hours too soon than a minute too late.

William Shakespeare

Keep strong, if possible. In any case, keep cool. Have unlimited patience. Never corner an opponent, and always assist him to save his face. Put yourself in his shoes—so as to see things through his eyes.

Basil Henry Liddell Hart

If you aren't fired with enthusiasm, you'll be fired with enthusiasm.

Vince Lombardi

If I had my life to live over, I'd like to make more mistakes next time. I would climb more mountains and swim more rivers. I would eat more ice cream and less beans. I would perhaps have more actual troubles, but fewer imaginary ones.

Nadine Stair

THE BODY

And in man or woman a clean, strong
Firm-fibred body is more beautiful than
the most beautiful face.

Walt Whitman

Fortunately for us and our world, youth is not easily
discouraged. Youth with its clear vista and boundless
faith and optimism is uninhibited by the thousands of
considerations that always bedevil man in his progress.
The hopes of the world rest on the flexibility, vigor,
capacity for new thought, the fresh outlook of the
young.

Dwight D. Eisenhower

The trouble with life in the fast lane is that you get to
the other end in an awful hurry.

John Jensen

We should conduct ourselves not as if we ought to live for the body, but as if we could not live without it.

Seneca

Smoking shortens your life by eight years. I love watching pro football on television. If I smoke, I'll miss 350 games.

Tony Curtis

Never eat more than you can lift.

Miss Piggy

Kids will eat mud (raw or baked), rocks, paste, crayons, ballpoint pens, moving goldfish, cigarette butts, and cat food. But try to coax a little beef stew into their mouths and they look at you like a puppy when you stand over him with the Sunday paper rolled up.

Erma Bombeck

If you don't think too good, don't think too much.

Ted Williams

Don't be frightened if things seem difficult in the beginning . . . the important thing is not to retreat; you have to master yourself. This ability to conquer oneself is no doubt the most precious of all the things sports bestows upon us.

Olga Korbut

Procrastination is the art of keeping up with yesterday.

Don Marquis

The man who complains about the way the ball bounces is likely the one who dropped it.

Lou Holtz

It's what you learn after you know it all that counts.

Earl Weaver (also attributed to John Wooden)

The only thing we have to fear is fear itself.

Franklin D. Roosevelt

Courage is resistance to fear, mastery of fear, not absence of fear.

Mark Twain

Always do what you are afraid to do.

Ralph Waldo Emerson

A professional basketball player must be able to run six miles in a game, a hundred games a year—jumping and pivoting under constant physical contact. My body becomes so finely tuned that three days without workouts makes a noticeable difference in timing, wind, and strength. I believe that basketball is the most physically grueling of all professional sports.

Bill Bradley

MORE OF THE COACH'S CORNER

The coaches who burn themselves out are the ones who are always second-guessing themselves. The players respect a coach who's not wishy-washy. It gives them confidence to have a leader who has no doubt in his mind once a decision is made about which way he wants to go.

Joe Greene

I quit coaching because of illness and fatigue. The fans were sick and tired of me.

John Ralston

When I coached at Niagara, we gave recruits a piece of caramel candy. If they took the wrapper off before eating it, they got a basketball scholarship; otherwise, they got a football scholarship.

Frank Layden

Every winning player wants to be disciplined, but they will test you. Some guys will test you for two days, some guys will test you for a week, some guys will test you the whole year. That's why you've got to be consistent with your discipline.

Bob Hill

Coaches who can outline plays on a blackboard are a dime a dozen. The ones who win get inside their players and motivate.

Vince Lombardi

Reality is something you rise above.

Liza Minnelli

The ultimate measure of a man is not where he stands in moments of comfort and convenience, but where he stands at times of challenge and controversy.

Martin Luther King Jr.

Fatigue makes cowards of us all.

Vince Lombardi

Success is that old ABC—ability, breaks, and courage.

Charles Luckman

Competition

The first and great commandment is "Don't let them scare you."

Elmer Davis

Nobody ever said, "Work ball!" They say, "Play ball!"
To me, that means having fun.

Willie Stargell

Be not afraid of greatness: some are born great, some
achieve greatness, and some have greatness thrust upon
them.

William Shakespeare

It ain't enough to get the breaks. You gotta know how to use 'em.

Huey P. Long

Coaches want to be in control. But the people we reward for making decisions are ultimately not in control. When the game begins, the athletes are on the field.

Todd Crossett

Things may come to those who wait, but only the things left by those who hustle.

Abraham Lincoln

See that dog there: he doesn't give a rat's behind about point average.

Arthur Channy character in Air Bud

Play like you've got guts coming out of your ears.

Paul "Bear" Bryant

The greatness of Michael Jordan is his competitive drive; the weakness of Michael Jordan is his competitive drive.

Phil Jackson

To set the cause above renown,
To love the game beyond the prize,
To honor, while you strike him down,
The foe that comes with fearless eyes;
To count the life of battle good
And dear the land that gave you birth,
And dearer yet the brotherhood
That binds the brave of all the earth.

Henry Newbolt

Smart is better than lucky.

Titanic Thompson

Sports are too hard to play unless they are played with joy.

Mel Allen

People are always blaming their circumstances for what they are. I don't believe in circumstances. The people who get on in this world are the people who get up and look for the circumstances they want, and if they can't find them, make them.

George Bernard Shaw

What got you here will get you out of here.

Joe Garagiola

If you make every game a life-and-death proposition, you're going to have problems. For one thing, you'll be dead a lot.

Dean Edwards Smith

I don't get consumed by circumstances that are beyond my control. If I worry, it beats everybody else down. I'm always into what's happening next. So Bob Griese has a broken ankle? OK, let's get Earl Morrall ready and put him in there.

Don Shula

If you want to win anything—a race, yourself, your life—you have to go a little berserk.

George Sheehan

It's not whether you get knocked down, it's whether you get up.

Vince Lombardi

Do not let what you cannot do interfere with what you can do.

John Wooden

BASEBALL

It's like church. Many attend, but few understand.

Wes Westrum

Baseball is almost the only orderly thing in a very unorderly world. If you get three strikes, even the best lawyer in the world can't get you off.

Bill Veeck

There are two theories on hitting the knuckleball. Unfortunately, neither of them works.

Charlie Lau

The way to catch a knuckleball is to wait until
the ball stops rolling and then pick it up.

Bob Uecker

Baseball players are the weirdest of all.
I think it's all that organ music.

Peter Gent

Baseball is a game of inches.

Branch Rickey

Never look behind you. Something may be gaining on you.

Satchel Paige

There's nothing mysterious about winning. It's a matter of executing the fundamentals.

Cal Ripken

Perseverance is more prevailing than violence; and many things which cannot be overcome when they are together, yield themselves up when taken little by little.

Plutarch

One man that has a mind and knows it can always beat ten men who haven't and don't.

George Bernard Shaw

We confide in our strength, without boasting of it; we respect that of others, without fearing it.

Thomas Jefferson

Show me a guy who's afraid to look bad, and I'll show you a guy you can beat every time.

Lou Brock

I give the same halftime speech over and over. It works best when my players are better than the other coach's players.

Chuck Mills

The strategy part is overrated. Every manager tries to give his players the chance to be successful.

Jim Leyland

Exercise equipment for sale. Fat guy wants money for
sofa.

Classified ad from the Sonora Union-Democrat,
October 29, 1990

It is often better not to see an insult, than to avenge it.

Seneca

In the field of sports you are more or less accepted for
what you do rather than what you are.

Althea Gibson

No matter how tough the situation looks, it's always
possible to succeed, as long as you give it an effort.

John Elway

The key is knowing how to peak.

Lasse Viren

NO POLE-VAULTING,
NO CROSS-COUNTRY RUNNING, AND
NO AWAY-GAMES.

Notice from the Activities Director,
State Correctional Institution at Pittsburgh

Doing your best at this moment puts you in the best place for the next moment.

Oprah Winfrey

Breaks balance out. The sun don't shine on the same ol' dog's ass every day.

Darrell Royal

Football is a game of errors. The team that makes the fewest errors in a game usually wins.

Paul Brown

AND MORE BASEBALL

The rhythms of the game are so similar to the patterns of American life. Periods of leisure, interrupted by bursts of frantic activity.

Roger Kahn

The secret of my success is clean living and a fast outfield.

Vernon "Lefty" Gomez

I hit 'em where they ain't.

Wee Willie Keeler

The charm of baseball is that, dull as it may be
on the field, it is endlessly fascinating as a rehash.

Jim Murray

Whoever wants to know the heart and mind of
America had better learn baseball, the rules and
realities of the game—and do it by watching first some
high-school or small-town teams.

Jacques Barzun

Never trust a baserunner who's limping. Comes a base hit and you'll think he just got back from Lourdes.

Joe Garagiola

Compete against yourself, not others.

Peggy Fleming

To win you have to risk loss.

Jean-Claude Killy

If there's one pitch you keep swinging at and keep missing, stop swinging at it.

Yogi Berra

It's not so important who starts the game, but who finishes it.

John Wooden

Winners never quit and quitters never win.

Anonymous

Most ball games are lost, not won.

Casey Stengel

I always have good finishes. You go as hard as you can until the end. You can always rest when it's over.

Janet Evans

If I were to try to read, much less answer, all the attacks made on me, this shop might as well be closed for any other business. I do the very best I know how—the very best I can; and I mean to keep doing so until the end. If the end brings me out all right, what is said against me won't amount to anything. If the end brings me out wrong, ten thousand angels swearing I was right would make no difference.

Abraham Lincoln

GOLF

I remember being upset once and telling my dad I wasn't following through right, and he replied, "Nancy, it doesn't make any difference to a ball what you do after you hit it."

Nancy Lopez

Lay off for a few weeks and then quit for good.

Sam Snead, advice to a novice golfer

There's no such thing as natural touch. Touch is something you create by hitting millions of golf balls.

Lee Trevino

Being left-handed is a big advantage: no one knows enough about your swing to mess you up with advice.

Bob Charles

If you are going to throw a club, it is important to throw it ahead of you, down the fairway, so you don't have to waste energy going back to pick it up.

Tommy Bolt

In case of a thunderstorm, stand in the middle of the fairway and hold up a one-iron. Not even God can hit a one-iron.

Lee Trevino

Golf matches are not won on the fairways or greens. They are won on the tee—the first one.

Bobby Riggs

The golf swing is like sex: you can't be thinking of the mechanics of the act while you're doing it.

Dave Hill

You never get ahead of anyone as long as you try to get even with him.

Lou Holtz

When the going gets tough, the tough get going.

Anonymous

For me, the fact that your game plan and strategies worked out—that's incidental. For me the satisfaction is that twelve guys have listened and absorbed, and found a way to band together to win.

Phil Jackson

You can't wring your hands and roll up your sleeves at the same time.

Michele Brown

When you get into a tight place and it seems that you can't go on, hold on—for that's just the place and the time that the tide will turn.

Harriet Beecher Stowe

Champions take responsibility. When the ball comes to the net, you can be sure I want the ball.

Billie Jean King

What difference does the uniform make? You don't hit with it!

Yogi Berra

When the blind man carries the lame man, both go forward.

Swedish proverb

Boys, baseball is a game where you gotta have fun.
You do that by winning.

Dave Bristol

Sweat is the cologne of accomplishment.

Heywood Hale Broun

There are two ways of exerting strength: one is
pushing down, the other is pulling up.

Booker T. Washington

The only way round is through.

Robert Frost

Don't be afraid to take a big step if one is indicated.
You can't cross a chasm in two small jumps.

David Lloyd George

The man who is swimming against the stream knows the strength of it.

Woodrow Wilson

The guts carry the feet, not the feet the guts.

Miguel de Cervantes

Use what you got, because that's all you get.

Clarence "Pine Top" Smith

Becoming number one is easier than staying number one.

Bill Bradley

Snowflakes are one of nature's most fragile things, but just look what they can do when they stick together.

Vesta M. Kelly

Before my opponent moves, I am already moving.

Chinese saying

Good teams become great ones when the members
trust each other enough to surrender the "me" for the
"we."

Phil Jackson

Take calculated risks. That is quite different than being
rash.

George S. Patton

Self-confidence is the first requisite to great
undertakings.

Samuel Johnson

In life as in football
Fall forward when you fall.

Arthur Guitterman

A wise man will make more opportunities than he finds.

Francis Bacon

You've got to know when to turn around.

John Roskelley

The art of running the mile consists, in essence, of reaching the threshold of unconsciousness at the instant of breasting the tape.

Paul O'Neil

Hope for the best. Expect the worst. Life is a play. We're unrehearsed.

Mel Brooks

After the Game

You can't win all the time. There are guys out there who are better than you.

Yogi Berra

What is defeat? Nothing but education, nothing but the first step toward something better.

Wendell Phillips

Success, n. More achievement than expectation.
Failure, n. More expectation than achievement.

Anonymous

Far better it is to dare mighty things, to win glorious triumphs, even though checkered by failure, than to take rank with those poor spirits who neither enjoy much nor suffer much, because they live in the gray twilight that knows not victory nor defeat.

Theodore Roosevelt

The spirit, the will to win, and the will to excel are the things that endure. These qualities are so much more important than the events that occur.

Vince Lombardi

I'm not afraid to lose and I'm not afraid to win.

Patty Sheehan

If you're old and you lose, they say you're outmoded. If you're young and you lose, they say you're green. So don't lose.

Terry Brennan

He who laughs, lasts.

Mary Pettibone Poole

What kills a skunk is the publicity it gives itself.

Abraham Lincoln

The only victory that counts is the one over yourself.

Jesse Owens

The important thing in the Olympic Games is not to win but to take part; the important thing in life is not the triumph but the struggle; the essential thing is not to have conquered but to have fought well.

Baron Pierre de Coubertin

Success is not forever, and failure isn't fatal.

Don Shula

CHARACTER

We aim to develop physique, mentality, and character in our students; but because the first two are menaces without the third, the greatest of these is character.

Joseph Dana Allen

I have never worked to be well-liked or well-loved, but only to be respected.

Bill Russell

The easiest thing in sport(s) is to win when you're good. The next easiest is to lose when you're not any good. The hardest is to lose when you're good. That's the test of character.

Roy Eisenhardt

Character is like a tree, and reputation like its shadow. The shadow is what we think of it; the tree is the real thing.

Anonymous

Be courageous. It's one of the only places left uncrowded.

Anita Roddick

To go against the dominant thinking of your friends, of most of the people you see every day, is perhaps the most difficult act of heroism you can have.

Theodore H. White

Leadership implies movement toward something, and convictions provide that direction. If you don't stand for something, you'll fall for anything.

Don Shula

Learn to say "No"—it will be of more use to you than to be able to read Latin.

Charles Haddon Spurgeon

There is the greatest practical benefit in making a few failures early in life.

T. H. Huxley

The human need to play is a powerful one. When we ignore it we feel there is something missing in our lives.

Anonymous

Don't go around saying the world owes you; the world owes you nothing, it was here first.

Mark Twain

If you can't stand the heat, get out of the kitchen.

Harry S. Truman

Blessed is he who expects nothing, for he shall never be disappointed.

Benjamin Franklin

You must have an alibi to show why you lost. If you haven't one, you must fake one. Your self-confidence must be maintained.

Christy Mathewson

Never lose track of what really matters in life. It doesn't matter how many points you score, or rebounds you grab, or games you win. In the end what will matter is the kind of father, son, brother, husband, or neighbor you are.

Charles Barkley

Happiness lies in the joy of achievement and the thrill of creative effort.

Franklin D. Roosevelt

Publicity is like poison: it doesn't hurt unless you swallow it.

Joe Paterno

I have always grown from my problems and challenges, from the things that don't work out. That's what I've really learned.

Carol Burnett

Be careful to get out of an experience all the wisdom that is in it—not like the cat that sits down on a hot stove. She will never sit down on a hot stove lid again—and that is well; but also she will never sit down on a cold one anymore.

Mark Twain

Life doesn't mean money. It doesn't mean success. It just means doing things as well as you can without worrying about anything else.

Terry Fox

Don't blame the lousy cabinets on the toolbox; just get back to work, fix it, do it right.

Andy Corbett

Winning is a habit. Unfortunately, so is losing.

Vince Lombardi

Failure is only the opportunity to begin again more intelligently.

Henry Ford

Try not to become a man of success, but rather try to become a man of value.

Albert Einstein

Don't measure yourself by what you have accomplished, but by what you should have accomplished with your ability.

John Wooden

Eating words has never given me indigestion.

Winston Churchill

Always forgive your enemies—nothing annoys them so much.

Oscar Wilde

You really never lose until you stop trying.

Mike Ditka

Keep your head up; act like a champion.

Paul "Bear" Bryant

Lots of people want to ride with you in the limo, but what you want is someone who will take the bus with you when the limo breaks down.

Oprah Winfrey

I don't think much of a man who is not wiser today than he was yesterday.

Abraham Lincoln

A life spent making mistakes is not only more honorable but more useful than a life spent doing nothing.

George Bernard Shaw

The greatest accomplishment is not in never failing, but in rising again after you fail.

Vince Lombardi

The world cares very little about what a man or woman knows; it's what the man or woman is able to do that counts.

Booker T. Washington

Whether it's politics or football, winning is like shaving: you do it every day or you wind up looking like a bum.

Jack Kemp

I have learned a philosophy in the great University of Hard Knocks. I have learned to live each day as it comes, and not to borrow trouble by dreading tomorrow.

Dorothea Dix

No one can make you feel inferior without your consent.

Eleanor Roosevelt

Winning isn't everything, but wanting to win is.

Vince Lombardi

O Captain! my Captain! our fearful trip is done,
The ship has weather'd every rack,
the prize we sought is won,
The port is near, the bells I hear, the
people all exulting.

Walt Whitman

You can't be brave if you've only had wonderful things
happen to you.

Mary Tyler Moore

The one serious conviction that a man should have is
that nothing should be taken too seriously.

Nicholas Murray Butler

In great attempts it is glorious even to fail.

Vince Lombardi

Don't find fault. Find a remedy.

Henry Ford

It's a lot tougher to be a football coach than a president.
You've got four years as president, and they guard you.
A coach doesn't have anyone to protect him when
things go wrong.

Harry S. Truman

Coach, someday when the going gets rough, tell the
boys to win one for the Gipper.

George Gipp, on his deathbed, to coach Knute Rockne

You're gonna lose some ball games and you're gonna
win some ball games, and that's about it.

Sparky Anderson

Mistakes are a part of the dues one pays for a full life.

Sophia Loren

If you can react the same way to winning and losing, that's a big accomplishment. That quality is important because it stays with you the rest of your life.

Chris Evert

There has never been a great athlete who dies not knowing what pain is.

Bill Bradley

To win, one must be big enough to see the worth in others, big enough to cheer when others score.

Lucie Campbell-Williams

The reward of a thing well done, is to have done it.

Ralph Waldo Emerson

To lose
Is to learn.

Anonymous

Experience is the worst teacher; it gives the test before presenting the lesson.

Vernon Law

There is nothing wrong with making mistakes. Just don't respond with encores.

Anonymous

One thorn of experience is worth a whole wilderness of warning.

James Russell Lowell

If a man aspires to the highest place, it is not dishonor to him to halt at the second, or even at the third.

Cicero

Criticism comes easier than craftsmanship.

Zeuxis

Press not a falling man too far.

William Shakespeare

When you win, nothing hurts.

Joe Namath

If you can meet with Triumph and Disaster
And treat those two impostors just the same . . .
If you can talk with crowds and keep your virtue,
Or walk with Kings—nor lose the common touch . . .
Yours is the Earth and everything that's in it,
And—which is more—you'll be a Man, my son!

Rudyard Kipling

AND MORE CHARACTER

The final forming of a person's character lies in their own hands.

Anne Frank

Talent develops in quiet places, character in the full current of human life.

Johann Wolfgang von Goethe

Always do right. It will gratify some people, and astonish the rest.

Mark Twain

If I take care of my character, my reputation will take care of itself.

Dwight L. Moody

74

Do all the good you can,
By all the means you can,
In all the ways you can,
In all the places you can,
At all the times you can,
To all the people you can,
As long as ever you can.

John Wesley

If it wasn't for my father, I think I might be in jail
now, not in the NBA. He always taught me to do the
right thing, to never forget my roots, to never forget
where I came from, and to never forget that I've been
fortunate.

Shaquille O'Neal

The only thing I ever thought about was to be as good
as I could. I never thought about being the greatest
baseball player or anything, just to be as good as I
could.

Hank Aaron

Fall seven times, stand up eight.

Japanese proverb

We do not stop playing because we grow old; we grow old because we stop playing.

Anonymous

How much easier it is to be critical than to be correct.

Benjamin Disraeli

Defeat is one thing; disgrace is another.

Winston Churchill

If a man has a talent and cannot use it, he has failed. If he has a talent and uses only half of it, he has partly failed. If he has a talent and learns somehow to use the whole of it, he has gloriously succeeded, and won a satisfaction and a triumph few men ever know.

Thomas Wolfe

There is not greater glory for a man as long as he lives than that which he wins by his own hands and feet.

Homer, The Odyssey

You always pass failure on the way to success.

Mickey Rooney

For when the One Great Scorer comes to write against your name, He marks—not that you won or lost—it's how you played the game.

Grantland Rice

Index of Sources

Berra, Yogi, American
baseball player, manager,
and coach (b. 1925), 46,
51,57

Berry, Chuck, American
singer and songwriter (b.
1926), 22

Blanchard, Ken, American
management consultant
and author,
18

Bolt, Tommy, American
professional golfer (b.
1916), 49

Bombeck, Erma, American
columnist, author, and
humorist (1927–1996), 11,
27

Bouton, Jim, American
baseball player,
sportscaster, and author
(b. 1939), 9

Bradley, Bill, American
politician and basketball
player (b. 1943), 29, 53,
71

Brennan, Terry, 58

Bristol, Dave, American
baseball manager, 52

Brock, Lou, American
baseball player and
broadcaster (b. 1939), 41

Brooks, Mel, American
actor, director, and
screenwriter (b. 1926),
55

Broun, Heywood Hale,
American author,
broadcaster, and actor (b.
1918), 5, 52

Brown, H. Jackson, Jr.,
American author (b.
1940), 6

Brown, Michele, 50

About the Authors

Jess Brallier and Sally Chabert, husband and wife, are the authors or coauthors of more than thirty books, including *Lawyers and Other Reptiles*, *The Jacks Book*, *The Wit and Wisdom of Medicine*, *The Hot Dog Cookbook*, *Presidential Wit and Wisdom*, *This Book Really Sucks*, and *The Cocktail Hour*. Brallier and Chabert don't coach; they can't even housebreak their dog. They live in Massachusetts with their two children.